THIS BOOK BELONGS TO

Jovie Finefrock

Blessings From

Your Holy Cross Family

Do not be anxious about anything,
but in everything, by prayer
and petition, with thanksgiving,
present your requests to God.

PHILIPPIANS 4:6 (NIV)

" Grow in the grace
and knowledge of
Our Lord and Savior
Jesus Christ.
To Him be the glory both
now and forever. Amen! "
2 Peter 3:18

This edition published 2006
Copyright © Concordia Publishing House
3558 S. Jefferson Avenue, St. Louis, MO 63118-3968
1-800-325-3040 • www.cph.org
The prayers in this book originally appeared in
God, I've Gotta Talk to You, Copyright © 1974 Concordia Publishing House.
God, I've Gotta Talk to You … Again, Copyright © 1985 Concordia Publishing House.
"About Me" on page 10 is from *More Songs of Gladness*,
Copyright © 1987 Concordia Publishing House
"When I Don't Feel Well" on page 20 is from *God's Children Pray*,
Copyright © 1989 Concordia Publishing House

Manufactured in China

1   2   3   4   5   6   7   8   9   10   15 14 13 12 11 10 09 08 07 06

Little Ones
Talk with God

A BOOK OF PRAYERS

Prayers are written by Walter Wangerin, Jr.,
John Paquette, Anne Jennings,
and Dan Carr

Illustrated by Sue Ramá

CONCORDIA PUBLISHING HOUSE · SAINT LOUIS

Dear Grown-Up,

Prayer is one of God's special gifts to His children. "Have faith in God," Jesus told Peter, "… whatever you ask in prayer, believe that you have received it, and it will be yours" (Mark 11:22–24).

Prayer is our opportunity to talk with our heavenly Father, to ask for His forgiveness, to thank and praise Him, and to ask for His help in our lives and in the lives of others. He will hear us and will answer our prayers in His own way and in His own wisdom and in His own time.

There are times when children's hearts are so full that they spontaneously spill over into prayers. There are times when children take great joy in repeating the words of familiar prayers—"Now I Lay Me," "Tender Jesus, Meek and Mild," and of course, "Our Father." But there are also times when the words don't come as easily and when a prayer just for children in a specific situation works best. Then it is a comfort to read a prayer about being lonely or afraid or about having hurt someone else.

Help your little one understand that there are many ways to pray: in groups or alone, in shouts or whispers, in songs or in thoughts. Pray often for and with your child and for yourself. "Rejoice always, pray without ceasing, give thanks in all circumstances; for this is the will of God in Christ Jesus for you" (1 Thessalonians 5:16–18). And assure your child that we have God's certain promise that He always hears and answers our prayers.

Our Father who art in heaven
hallowed be Thy name,
Thy kingdom come,
Thy will be done
on earth as it is in heaven.
Give us this day our daily bread;
and forgive us our trespasses
as we forgive those
who trespass against us;
and lead us not into temptation,
but deliver us from evil.
For Thine is the kingdom
and the power and the glory
forever and ever. Amen.

In the Morning

Dear God, I thank You for this day
    That's only just begun,
The pearly dew upon the grass,
    The newly risen sun.
Be with me in the busy hours
    And lay Your hand in mine.
Please let the path I walk be bright,
    With loving deeds ashine.
Teach me to know You and to pray.
Dear God, I thank You for this day.

At Meals

Our health is given by this food;
Our food, dear Lord, comes by Thy grace.
Our thanks we offer in return
At every meal, in every place.

Dear God, we thank You for this food
    As well as we are able.
Please bless it, Father, for our use,
    And be our Guest at table.

About Me

Thank You, God, for sky and sea.
Thank You, God, for making me.

You gave me lungs so I could breathe.
You gave me a nose so I could sneeze.
You gave me a mind so I could think.
You gave me eyes so I could blink.

You gave me a home, my mom and dad.
And friends and pets. And am I glad!
You gave me a heart that beats in love
For things on earth and You above.

Thank You, God, for sky and sea.
Thank You, God, for making me. Amen.

(From *More Songs of Gladness*)

I Like

There are lots of things I like,
And here are just a few:
Snakes and spiders, bats and lizards.
    Thanks God—You made them, too!

About My Family

F ather gives me love so true,

A nd mom keeps me in her prayers

M y brothers and sisters too—

I know they really, really care.

L ord, let them know I love them, too.

Y our love's the key; we learn from You.

About My Friends

I thank You, Father, for my friends,
    Who are so close to me.
We laugh and play; at school we work
    So very busily.
I thank You for Your gracious love,
    Which never has an end.
But most, I thank You for Your Son,
    My Savior and my Friend.

About Sick People

Hear my prayer, Lord, for the ill:

Encourage them while they lie still

And through Your Word let their spirits rest.

Lead them through the painful night,

Through fevers, needles, dreams, and fright;

Heal their bodies, their spirits bless.

When I Don't Feel Well

I don't feel well;
This is no fun.
I am so sick today.
Dear Jesus,
Help me know Your love,
And comfort me, I pray. Amen.

Questions

How far is far?
How cold is cold?
How young is young?
How old is old?
How rich is rich?
How poor is poor?
How bad is bad?
How pure is pure?

Oh, there are lots of questions, God,
I don't have answers to;
So, help me always to believe
And put my trust in You.

The Bible says You took my sin.
You died at Calvary
So, that is why I never doubt
You hear my every prayer.

About School

Suddenly summer is no longer here.

Christ, come with me in Your Word this year:

Hands raised to answer questions wrong or right,

Old friends and new, and homework for the night,

Our teacher, paper, pens—it all is new.

Lord, in my learning now I thank You.

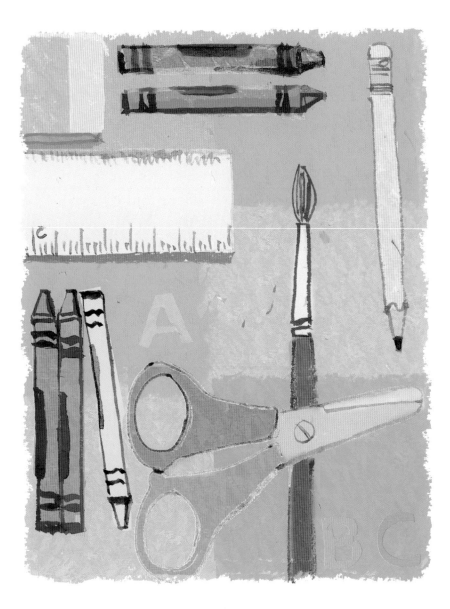

Fun

It's fun to run and jump and roll
    Down hills so bright and green.
It's fun to swim and float and dive
    In waters cool and clean.

It's fun to walk and skip and sing
    Without a single care.
It's fun, when at the end of day
    I say my bedtime prayers.

I have fun almost anywhere
    Because I am Your own;
Your special, loved, forgiven child,
    Through Jesus Christ alone.

I'm Sorry

A strange thing, Jesus, makes me cry—
When someone *else* is hurt and I,
I know *I* hurt that other guy,
    His hurt becomes my own.
But Peter hurt You, didn't he?
And You forgave him, set him free.
So, Jesus, You remember me;
    For my sin You did atone.
Please help my friend forgive my sin
And make us then what we have been—
    Two friends who love like one.

When I'm Not Nice

It wasn't very nice of me
    To say the things I did.
But, God, You've got to understand—
    He's such a nasty kid!

I try to be good all the time.
    But God, sometimes I don't.
It is my sin. I can't blame him.
    Next time, I'll watch my tone.

Lord, I know that no one's perfect.
    (Except for Jesus, that is.)
And since He died for all our sins,
    I pray, Lord, please forgive.

When I'm Afraid

I couldn't count, dear Lord, the things
    That sometimes frighten me:
An open window five floors up,
    The deep holes in the sea,
The dogs who flash their teeth by day,
    The darkness of the night,
And death, and life, and things to come,
    Things loud like dynamite.
But none of these can separate
    Me, Jesus, from Your love,
For You are with me here below
    While You're with God above.

Dear God

Dear God, You made the mountains high;
    You made the bubbly seas.
You made the pretty butterflies
    And the busy bumble bees.

You made the tiny grains of sand;
    You made the big tall trees.
And then, Lord, with Your loving hands
    You made a child named me.

My Friends Won't Let Me Play

I watched my friends all playing ball.
    I wanted to play, too.
They said, "Although you wish you could,
    There is no place for you."

I felt like crying. I was sad.
    I hurt real bad inside.
But so they wouldn't see me cry,
    I found a place to hide.

When your friends ran off and left You,
    Lord, You were lonely, too.
But, You forgave them—every one—
    For that's what friends all do.

I know, Lord, what You did then—
    You died, but now You live.
And that is why I ask You now,
    To help me to forgive.

When I'm Happy

Times come, dear Jesus, when my smile
Stretches like rubber for half a mile;
And then it breaks and then I laugh
So hard it aches for a day and a half.
I laugh at anything, I guess—
At leaves, at lunch, at words like "yes."
Thanks, Lord, for Your gift of happiness.

God Bless My Friend

I know You hear me when I pray,
　　Because my sins are washed away.
So, can I tell You, God, what happened
　　To my friend today?

He raced his bike along the road
　　So fast he made a breeze
When, suddenly, he hit a rock
　　And fell and hurt his knees.

He cried because it hurt a lot.
　　I cried because I care.
And now You know, dear Jesus, why
　　I come to You in prayer.

Please dry his tears, dear Jesus, Lord,
　　And let him know You care.
Please heal his knees so we can ride
　　Together everywhere.

About Forgiveness

F ind me, Lord; I'm small as a pin.

O h, gracious God forgive my sin!

R emind me of Your great commands,

G ive me peace in Your loving hands—

I 'm small, I'm sinful, and I'm here,

V ery unhappy, full of fear.

E ach sin, Lord, I know You see.

M y Savior, find me, set me free.

E very day, I'm loved by Thee!

About the Seasons

Sometimes I run with my arms wide apart,
Green grass on my feet and joy in my heart.
Sometimes I leap into brown autumn leaves;
I crunch them and punch them;
    I breathe them and sneeze.
Sometimes I give the cold snow a good place
To land on in winter: my hands and my face.
Then in spring, we rejoice in the victory,
That You, Lord Jesus won over death for me.

About Forgiving Others

Lord, on the cross You were hurting
  Through and through—
Cuts in Your feet, Your side, Your hands,
  Your head—
You looked on those who did this thing to You
And cried for them, and this is what You said:
"Forgive them for they know not what they do."
Oh, Jesus, sometimes people hurt me too.
Teach me to look on them with peace, with love,
Forgiving them as You forgive above.

God's Beautiful World

The sky is blue, the grass is green,
    The flowers are in bloom.
The trees reach up into the sky,
    The clouds look like balloons.

I am so happy to be here,
    Where Christ came from above,
To die on a cross for all our sin,
    And rose to show His love.

I cannot make a tree or cloud;
    I cannot make the sea.
But most of all I'm happy, Lord,
    That You gave Your life for me.

Treasures

I found the neatest things today
    Just lying on the ground:
The feather of a pretty bird,
    An acorn, big and brown.

That bird has flown up in the sky;
    I'd like to fly along.
That acorn's just a bit like me:
    We'll both grow big and strong.

You made all things, God, that I know.
    You made my friends, my folks, and me!
Thank You, God, for making sure
    From sins Christ sets us free.

When I'm Lonely

Times come, dear Jesus, when I find
No one's here to play with me.
My friends aren't home. I'm left behind.
I'm sad and mad and lonely.
Dear Jesus, You were once alone.
On the cross, You hung and died.
And still You love and You atone.
Dear Lord, You're at my side.
Even when I'm by myself, I know
Jesus loves me, loves me so!

When I Grow Up

Sometimes it's very clear to me
    Exactly what I'm going to be:
Teacher, lawyer, merchantman,
    An astronaut or fireman.
But now and then I get confused;
    I'm not quite sure just what to choose.
I know I won't go far alone,
    So, help me, Lord, before I'm grown.

At Night

The night is dark and silent now;
Lord, let my sleep tonight endow
With Your peace and blessedness.
Lord, keep me safe and give me rest,
And when the morning comes to light,
Keep me in Your grace and might.

Then you will call upon Me and come and pray to Me, and I will hear you.

JEREMIAH 29:12